D0708232

'RE LI...

524 775 71 4

THE WORLD'S WORST NATURAL DISASTERS

THE WORLD'S WORST
FLOODS

by John R. Baker

raintree
a Capstone company — publishers for children

Raintree is an imprint of Capstone Global Library Limited, a company incorporated in England and Wales having its registered office at 264 Banbury Road, Oxford, OX2 7DY – Registered company number: 6695582

www.raintree.co.uk
myorders@raintree.co.uk

Text © Capstone Global Library Limited 2017
The moral rights of the proprietor have been asserted.

All rights reserved. No part of this publication may be reproduced in any form or by any means (including photocopying or storing it in any medium by electronic means and whether or not transiently or incidentally to some other use of this publication) without the written permission of the copyright owner, except in accordance with the provisions of the Copyright, Designs and Patents Act 1988 or under the terms of a licence issued by the Copyright Licensing Agency, Saffron House, 6–10 Kirby Street, London EC1N 8TS (www.cla.co.uk). Applications for the copyright owner's written permission should be addressed to the publisher.

Edited by Aaron Sautter
Designed by Steve Mead
Picture research by Jo Miller
Production by Tori Abraham
Originated by Capstone Global Library Limited
Printed and bound in China

ISBN 978 1 474 72477 7
20 19 18 17 16
10 9 8 7 6 5 4 3 2 1

British Library Cataloguing in Publication Data
A full catalogue record for this book is available from the British Library.

Acknowledgements
We would like to thank the following for permission to reproduce photographs: AP Images: The Southern Illinoisan/Paul Newton, 12–13; Corbis, 8–9, 20–21, Andrew Holbrooke, 10–11; Gamma-Rapho via Getty Images: Chip HIRES, 22–23; Getty Images: AFP/STR, 26–27; iStockphoto: RonBailey, 28–29; Newscom: EPA/POOL/Vincent Laforet, 14–15, Mondadori/Giorgio Lotti, 16–17, ZUMA Press/KEYSTONE Pictures USA, 24–25; NOAA/National Weather Service Collection, 18–19; Shutterstock: Brisbane, design elements, leonello calvetti, cover, 3, 31, Lisa S., cover, Vladimir Melnikov, 4–5, xpixel, design elements; The Image Works: Lebrecht, 6–7

Every effort has been made to contact copyright holders of material reproduced in this book. Any omissions will be rectified in subsequent printings if notice is given to the publisher.

All the internet addresses (URLs) given in this book were valid at the time of going to press. However, due to the dynamic nature of the internet, some addresses may have changed, or sites may have changed or ceased to exist since publication. While the author and publisher regret any inconvenience this may cause readers, no responsibility for any such changes can be accepted by either the author or the publisher.

CONTENTS

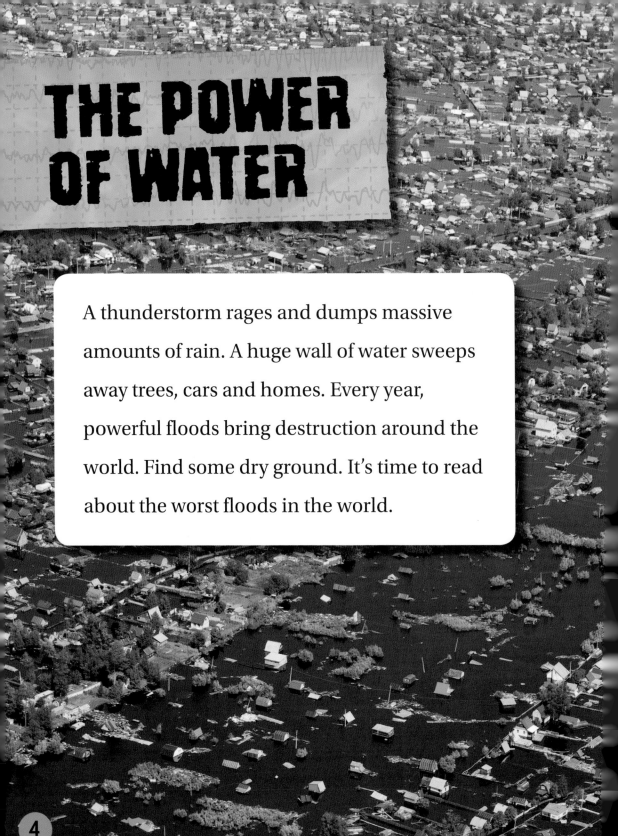

THE POWER OF WATER

A thunderstorm rages and dumps massive amounts of rain. A huge wall of water sweeps away trees, cars and homes. Every year, powerful floods bring destruction around the world. Find some dry ground. It's time to read about the worst floods in the world.

TYPES OF FLOOD

Floods come in many forms. However they arrive, floods overwhelm land that is normally dry.

FLASH FLOOD:

A stream or river rises quickly and pours over its banks. It's usually caused by heavy rain or a **dam** bursting.

URBAN FLOOD:

Heavy rain overwhelms city drainage systems and turns roads into rivers.

REGIONAL FLOOD:

A big river overflows its banks. It covers a large area with water for a long period of time.

ICE JAM FLOOD:

Huge chunks of ice clog a river, causing water to overflow.

STORM SURGE FLOOD:

A hurricane or strong storm pushes seawater inland.

dam barrier built to hold back a body of water

HISTORY'S DEADLIEST FLOOD

Location:
northern China

Date:
summer 1931

Area covered:

square miles	square kilometres
40,000	100,000
35,000	90,000
30,000	80,000
	70,000
25,000	60,000
20,000	50,000
15,000	40,000
	30,000
10,000	20,000
5,000	10,000
0	0

During the summer of 1931, heavy rainfall sent China's Huang He River flowing over its banks. The flood covered thousands of square kilometres. It ruined crops and spread disease. It claimed the lives of about 4 million people.

FACT

China's massive 1931 flood left more than 80 million people without homes.

MISSISSIPPI RIVER DISASTER

Location:
Mississippi River
Valley, USA

Date:
spring and
summer 1927

Area covered:

square miles	square kilometres
40,000	100,000
35,000	90,000
30,000	80,000
25,000	70,000
20,000	60,000
15,000	50,000
10,000	40,000
5,000	30,000
0	20,000
	10,000
	0

Heavy spring rains in 1927 caused the Mississippi River to reach **flood stage**. The water broke **levees** that protected towns and farms. Floodwaters covered millions of hectares of land. The water damaged 162,000 homes. More than 240 people died.

flood stage level a river or stream reaches when it begins to cause damage

levee bank of earth or structure built at the side of a river to keep it from overflowing

GREAT FLOOD OF 1993

Location:
Upper Mississippi
River, USA

Date:
summer 1993

Area covered:

square miles	square kilometres
40,000	100,000
35,000	90,000
30,000	80,000
	70,000
25,000	60,000
20,000	50,000
15,000	40,000
10,000	30,000
	20,000
5,000	10,000
0	0

FACT

The 1993 Mississippi River flood damaged or destroyed more than 50,000 homes.

Another major flood occurred along the upper Mississippi River in 1993. It covered 78,000 square kilometres (30,000 square miles) in the north-central United States. The floodwaters caused $20 billion worth of damage.

MANAGING A MAJOR FLOOD

Location:
Lower Mississippi River, USA

Date:
April to June 2011

Area covered:

square miles	square kilometres
40,000	100,000
35,000	90,000
30,000	80,000
	70,000
25,000	60,000
20,000	50,000
15,000	40,000
10,000	30,000
	20,000
5,000	10,000
0	0

In 2011 heavy rains swelled the Ohio and Mississippi Rivers in the USA. To save Cairo, Illinois, engineers blew up a levee. This redirected the floodwaters. In Morganza, Louisiana, they opened **spillway** gates. This helped to prevent flooding in the city.

In 2011, floodwaters along the lower Mississippi River lasted from April to June. The water reached record levels at Vicksburg and Natchez, Mississippi.

spillway structure or passage allowing excess water to move from the main river to another area in order to lower the water level

WHEN THE LEVEES BROKE

Location:
New Orleans,
Louisiana, USA

Date:
29 August 2005

Peak water height:

feet	metres
40	12
35	10
30	8
25	
20	6
15	4
10	2
5	
0	0

Hurricane Katrina roared into New Orleans on 29 August 2005. The storm's 5.8-metre (19-foot) **storm surge** broke through levees. The city was flooded. Thousands of people huddled on roofs and in trees waiting to be rescued.

FACT

After the hurricane, water covered 80 per cent of New Orleans. It was up to 6 metres (20 feet) deep in some places.

storm surge huge wave of water pushed ashore by an approaching hurricane

FLORENCE UNDER WATER

Location:
Florence, Italy

Date:
4 November 1966

Peak water height:

In 1966, three days of heavy rain turned the River Arno into a **torrent**. The water reached up to 3 metres (10 feet) high as it raged through Florence, Italy. The flood killed about 100 people. It left 5,000 families homeless.

feet	metres
40	12
35	10
30	
25	8
20	6
15	4
10	
5	2
0	0

FACT

Florence was famous for its artwork and books. The flood damaged or destroyed millions of rare books and works of art. Some of them were repaired. Others were lost forever.

torrent strong, fast-moving stream of water or other liquid

BLACK HILLS FLOOD

Location:
Rapid City, South Dakota, USA

Date:
9 June 1972

Peak water height:

feet	metres
40	12
35	10
30	
25	8
20	6
15	4
10	
5	2
0	0

On 9 June 1972, 38 centimetres (15 inches) of rain fell over the Black Hills of South Dakota, USA. Rapid Creek became a raging river. Then a nearby dam broke. A flash flood ripped through Rapid City. The flood destroyed 15 bridges. It ruined more than 1,000 homes.

FACT

The Black Hills flood killed 238 people. It caused more than $165 million in damage.

DEADLIEST US FLOOD

Location:
Johnstown,
Pennsylvania, USA

Date:
31 May 1889

Peak water height:

feet	metres
40	12
35	10
30	8
25	
20	6
15	4
10	2
5	
0	0

The deadliest flood in US history hit Johnstown, Pennsylvania, on 31 May 1889. Heavy rains and rising water burst a nearby dam. The wall of water ripped apart homes, barns and bridges. The disaster destroyed about 1,600 homes. It killed 2,209 people.

FACT

Up to 18 million tonnes of water flowed through Johnstown in the 1889 flood.

BANGLADESH DISASTER

Location:
Bangladesh

Date:
July to September 1998

Area covered:

square miles	square kilometres
40,000	100,000
35,000	90,000
30,000	80,000
	70,000
25,000	60,000
20,000	50,000
15,000	40,000
	30,000
10,000	20,000
5,000	10,000
0	0

During the summer of 1998, much of Bangladesh was under water. Heavy **monsoon** rains caused severe flooding of the country's main rivers. The water ruined much of the food supply. Water wells became dirty. Disease spread quickly.

FACT

The flood in Bangladesh left between 21 and 25 million people homeless.

monsoon seasonal wind pattern that helps create heavy rainfall at certain times of the year

NORTH SEA TRAGEDY

Location:
Netherlands, UK, Belgium

Date:
1 February 1953

Area covered:

square miles	square kilometres
40,000	100,000
35,000	90,000
30,000	80,000
	70,000
25,000	60,000
20,000	50,000
15,000	40,000
	30,000
10,000	20,000
5,000	10,000
0	0

tide rising and falling of the sea up and down the shore

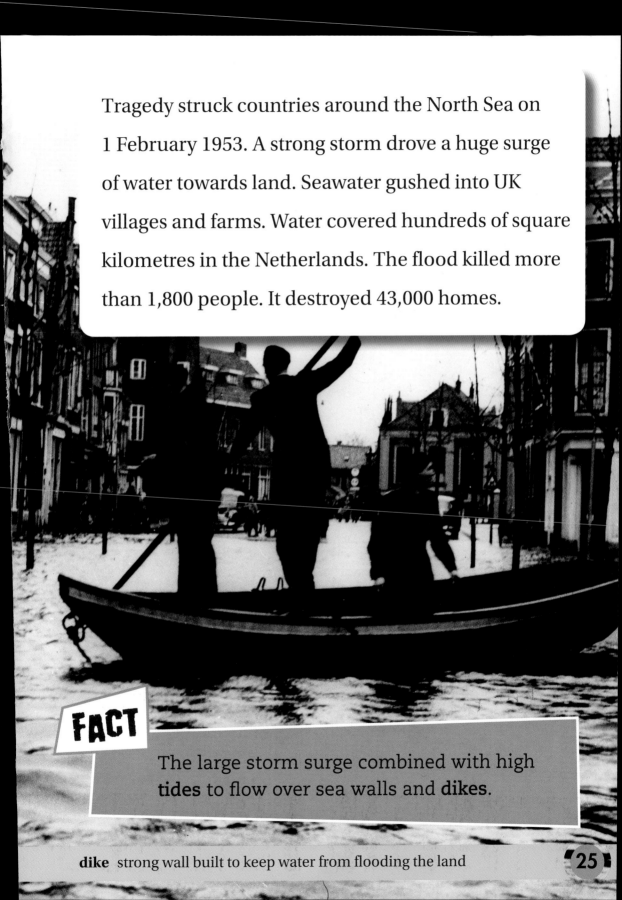

Tragedy struck countries around the North Sea on 1 February 1953. A strong storm drove a huge surge of water towards land. Seawater gushed into UK villages and farms. Water covered hundreds of square kilometres in the Netherlands. The flood killed more than 1,800 people. It destroyed 43,000 homes.

FACT

The large storm surge combined with high **tides** to flow over sea walls and **dikes**.

dike strong wall built to keep water from flooding the land

BANQUIAO DAM DISASTER

Location:
China

Date:
8 August 1975

Peak water height:

feet	metres
40	12
35	10
30	8
25	
20	6
15	4
10	
5	2
0	0

In 1975, **super-typhoon** Nina dropped more than 102 centimetres (40 inches) of rain on China. The Banquiao Dam burst on 8 August. The wall of water was up to 11 kilometres (7 miles) wide and 10 metres (33 feet) high. It wiped out entire villages. Water covered millions of hectares of land.

FACT

More than 60 other dams failed in the disaster. The flood destroyed 6 million buildings. It killed 85,600 people. About 140,000 more people died later from disease and a lack of food.

super-typhoon large spinning storm in the north-west Pacific Ocean with sustained winds of 241 kilometres (150 miles) per hour or more

STAYING SAFE IN A FLOOD

It's important to know what to do if a flood threatens your area. Try to get to higher ground. Stay away from flooded areas. The water can quickly sweep you off your feet. Floods can be dangerous. Stay safe by keeping calm and knowing what to do.

DISASTER EMERGENCY KIT

An emergency kit can be very helpful in case of a flood. A good kit should include these items:

- ✔ first-aid kit
- ✔ torch
- ✔ battery-powered radio
- ✔ extra batteries
- ✔ blankets

- ✔ bottled water
- ✔ tinned and dried food
- ✔ tin opener
- ✔ whistle to alert rescue workers

GLOSSARY

dam barrier built to hold back a body of water

dike strong wall built to keep water from flooding the land

flood stage level a river or stream reaches when it begins to cause damage

levee bank of earth or structure built on the side of a river to keep it from overflowing

monsoon seasonal wind pattern that helps create heavy rainfall at certain times of the year

spillway structure or passage allowing excess water to move from the main river to another area in order to lower the water level

storm surge huge wave of water pushed ashore by an approaching hurricane

super-typhoon large spinning storm in the north-west Pacific Ocean with sustained winds of 241 kilometres (150 miles) per hour or more

tide rising and falling of the sea up and down the shore

torrent strong, fast-moving stream of water or other liquid

READ MORE

Floods: Be Aware and Prepare (Weather Aware), Renée Gray-Wilburn (Capstone Press, 2014)

Surviving Floods (Children's True Stories: Natural Disasters), Elizabeth Raum (Raintree, 2012)

Storms and Hurricanes, Emily Bone (Usborne Publishing, 2012)

WEBSITES

www.dkfindout.com/uk/earth/earthquakes/tsunami

Found out more about tsunamis and how they are caused.

news.bbc.co.uk/cbbcnews/hi/find_out/guides/world/floods/newsid_1613000/1613858.stm

Discover more about flooding, following news stories from around the world.

COMPREHENSION QUESTIONS

1. Floods can be deadly and incredibly destructive. How many people died in the deadliest flood ever recorded?

2. Explain what you should do if a flood threatens your area.

3. Describe the different kinds of flood and how each occurs.

INDEX